CW00666376

REALITY CHECK

A SIMPLE GUIDE TO FINAL ENLIGHTENMENT

HELEN HAMILTON

BALBOA.PRESS

A DIVISION OF HAY HOUSE

Balboa Press books may be ordered through booksellers or by contacting:

Balboa Press
A Division of Hay House
1663 Liberty Drive
Bloomington, IN 47403
www.balboapress.co.uk
UK TFN: 0800 0148647 (Toll Free inside the UK)
UK Local: 02036 956325 (+44 20 3695 6325 from outside the UK)

Print information available on the last page.

ISBN: 978-1-9822-8317-9 (sc)
ISBN: 978-1-9822-8318-6 (e)

Balboa Press rev. date: 02/22/2021

CONTENTS

DEDICATION

This book is dedicated to making the first and last duality easy to transcend. It is not hard and neither should it take a long time to realise the truth. May you find the peace that you are looking for in the true understanding and direct experience of reality.

CHAPTER 1

Introduction

You are the formless reality in which the universe is simply an appearance and not an actual thing. There are no actual things, everything that appears to be tangible and solid is really only so because we are perceiving it through our human senses. What is real is the formless, intangible Self that is everywhere at all times. You are not a human being and you are not the formless cause of all the forms.

There is no manifestation of this world, things, objects and people; it is all the One Self. Many spiritual students struggle with trying to understand how the manifest and unmanifest can be really the same thing and spend a lot of wasted energy trying to resolve this. This book will help you to come to understand reality as it really is.

Some of the ideas in this book will seem impossible to understand at first but with repetition they will begin to make sense. To perceive reality directly is to understand what you really are and what everything is. Once you really understand what you are, then nothing will be confusing anymore and you will be able to read the statements above and they will seem obvious. You will wonder how you ever thought that you were a separate and limited human being, destined to be born, to live and to die.

How can you come to know that you are present everywhere and at all times? How can you come to know beyond a doubt that you are infinite and unlimited? How can you shed the thoughts and assumptions that the mind uses to keep you feeling bound? We will take a journey of realisations, insights and understandings in this book that can help you undo the assumptions that are stopping your eternal joy. With each chapter we will undo more of the assumptions of the mind and it will become clearer and clearer what you are. If you do not understand something written in the upcoming chapters, know that you have infinite help around you, even if you are alone reading this and do not know of anyone else that is like you and interested in truth. Simply the wish to understand it must bring that understanding to you in time and you can always re-read each chapter until it makes sense.

The truth of your being and the truth of what reality is are the same thing. You are reality. You are everywhere at all times. Time and space exist only as an idea inside you. It is time to break free from all limitations and to begin to live as your infinite Self. Mind is hypnotic and alluring for a limited time only — the fact that you are reading this means it is losing its hold over you. There is a whole reality beyond the mind and that IS what you are.

There will be times when you doubt if you can do this, whether you can understand this, but remember you can always contact us to ask questions or get help. Contact details are in the back of the book. Now let's get started!

Read this book in its entirety a few times. We learn by repetition and we only accept that as true that seems obvious and familiar to us. It is up to you to read this and question what you read consistently enough to make it your own direct knowledge and experience. If there is any "gap" between what you have seen to be true and what you are living as then there MUST be a belief in the way that needs to be removed.

Simply to recognise "I don't understand what has been written, but I would like to know it beyond doubt" will bring that to you. Ask that question and go have a cup of tea and watch the understanding present itself to you.

Always rely on your own experience of what is written here. Do not be content with my words. Become this book. Live as this book and you will never know suffering again.

CHAPTER 2

Discovering That You Are Formless

This chapter will help you to discover what you really are and it will begin to undo some of the main assumptions in our thinking process that keep us from seeing clearly. We will use the time old process of self-enquiry to begin to understand what we are.

Self-enquiry is simply when we actually look at what we are, rather than thinking about it. It is where we directly experience what we actually are which is important because our mind cannot get in the way of this process. If you sit here and think "I am the unlimited reality that is infinite and all-pervading" then it will not help you unless you actually directly come to know that beyond just thinking about it. Only by directly experiencing what you really are will you begin to see clearly. If we merely think about this, then our assumptions about ourselves will alter what we perceive.

Whatever we believe to be true about ourselves, the world and life, we will directly experience as very real indeed. Most of us believe that we are separate human beings, born and due to live for a certain number of years before we die and this is what we experience as real. The actuality of our existence is very different though and we must come to know it without relying on thoughts. There is nothing wrong with thoughts at all — many processes and issues in our daily life require a logical thought process; but to awaken fully to the reality of what you are, we need to put thought aside for a while.

Each thought we believe will begin to colour our experience of the truth just as sure as wearing coloured spectacles will colour the world we see with our eyes. When we consider that most of the thoughts we believe to be true are totally under our conscious radar and we do not know what they are, then we get into some very unreliable experiences of what truth is, what we are. It is necessary to always and only use your direct experience to verify what is true. We must be able to experience it and prove it within our own self so that we can know for certain it is true. Anything else is just adding to the mountain of thoughts that flies through most people's heads and will not help us. We do not need to stop thoughts nor eliminate the mind; in fact to try to do so will not help at all. We simply need to discern what answers we are willing to take as valid in our self-enquiry. So even if thoughts are there we can say "thank you very much, mind" and only accept a direct experience.

So self-enquiry is as simple as asking "what am I really"? and seeing what answer we find. We will always find thought answers of course and there is nothing wrong with these; mind will have many things to say about what we are. What can we experience directly though, is something very different to what you may have expected. What will you find from your self-enquiry? Nothing! You will experience nothing at all and this is the perfect answer.

When we self-enquire and ask what we really are, we may experience a vast space that seems empty, void and with no substance at all and it can seem unsettling or strange to us at first, perhaps even a little frightening. If we keep looking at that vastness, we begin to get used to it. This vast nothingness is what we really are, but it is not at all what we THOUGHT we are and so it will take some adjusting. This vast nothingness is not a thing at all, and it is most certainly not the "someone" we expected to find. It is formless and shapeless and yet it is very much present. Remember, we are only going to take our direct experience that we can know as truth here. Also remember here, that we are only just finding out now what we have always been; no matter how long we may have believed, assumed and experienced ourselves as separate and limited human beings, it has never been so. Never. You are now coming to see what you have always been.

Ask the question again and see what you find. You will find the same thing again and every single time you ask. It is just you and you are formless and everywhere. If you stay in that direct experience and ask some questions of yourself based on that nothingness you may be surprised at what you find.

- Are you tangible or intangible?
- Are you over here or over there?
- Do you have any shape or colour?
- Where exactly are you?
- Are you changing, growing, becoming, here as this vastness?
- What time is it in the vastness?
- How far do you reach and where do you end? Do you end at all?

7

- When did this vastness that you are, appear? When will it disappear?
- Were you born as this? When did you start?
- Is there you and another person here? Where do you stop and the person next to you start?

These questions may seem difficult to answer at first, but if you will continue to ask them you will soon find you begin to make some breakthroughs. As you go about your daily life you may notice that everything seems different now that you have seen what you really are. Our whole lives as human beings are based on the assumption that we are a separate person, a someone who is moving around in time and space and living out a life for 70, 80 or 90 years before we leave this planet. It can be quite a shock to realise that is not so.

Before we have fully understood what it means to be formless it may seem that life "out here" feels pointless and insignificant. You may find yourself wondering "what use is all this world, then"? "What is the reason for my existence if I am not what I thought I am"? If such feelings arise you can know that it is only a temporary phase of adjustment to your new way of perceiving yourself and that once you fully realise what you are, you will know the answer to these questions. As human beings we are taught to value the familiar, the known and the safe thoughts and when we suddenly find what we know to be challenged, we can feel insecure for a time. It can help to realise that what we thought we knew about ourselves was never actually true, but we have been fooled into thinking so. You are only coming to see how it has always been. It is safest to work from direct experience of what you can prove inside yourself rather than base your life on assumptions that have never been questioned until now.

Take some time to consider the questions listed in this chapter. Try to find an answer but do not worry if you cannot answer them all at this point. The answers will reveal themselves as you progress to the next chapters. Your understanding of what you are, what reality is, will deepen as you continue to read.

To continue to progress to the deeper stages of enlightenment we must be willing to realise that what we have called our life has been based on assumptions that are not true. We have based our whole existence on the idea that "I am so-and-so – a human being living in the world with family, friends, relationships, a job and an endpoint". For some people, it will take a while to come to terms with the fact that none of this has been true. You were never limited, lost or separate from everything and everyone. Some people that read this will immediately be unable to tolerate any lies within themselves about their origin and the nature of their existence and they will be driven by an urge to find out the whole truth and live as and from that truth. Others that read this will face too much resistance from their old and familiar ways of thinking about themselves and so may stop reading this, lose the book somehow or get distracted until a much later time. Any of these options is fine for once the truth has been revealed to you, it is only a matter of time before the want arises in you to fully comprehend what you are and what all this world is. This desire will become stronger until it seems to be the only thing that matters.

CHAPTER 3

What Does It Mean to Be Formless?

Most people that use self-enquiry do so to a certain point and then stop after a basic level of realisation of what we are. To fully understand what it means to be formless and to live as that is going to require you to challenge every assumption or thought you believe. It need not take a long time, nor need it be difficult if you are already willing to change the way you perceive the world, yourself and other beings. The aim of this book is to help you challenge every thought and assumption that is currently holding you in a limited perception of reality. You will have to be honest with yourself when an assumption pops up and you feel resistance to looking at it. You will also have to be honest with yourself if you find you are becoming distracted from this most vital work and realising what you truly are in its fullness.

Right now in this world there are thousands upon thousands of spiritual seekers who believe they know the full truth of what they are because they have seen what you have seen in the previous chapters. People will often say something like "I have seen what I really am, but I still have to live in the world", or "how do I live as this formlessness but still pay my bills and go to work"? Many times I hear people who say and believe they have fully realised the truth of what they are but they still deeply believe in an "out here" that is different to the reality of the formless Self. If you find this is still the case for you, then realisation is not yet complete. True knowing of the formlessness is to know yourself as all of Reality. There is no "world" or "manifest" or "reflection" external to the unmanifest awareness that you are. The full realisation of the absolute reality should and MUST permeate all of your life too and unless it does then it is not yet complete. What we call the outer world, the universe of solid objects is not how we think it is. No form, no body, no object is really there as we think it is and until this has been deeply assimilated you will continue to experience lack, limitation and suffering.

I will say that again because it contradicts so many of our cherished assumptions:

- The world is not different from or separate from the Self.
- The manifest did not ever arise out of the unmanifest.
- There is no difference between form and formless.
- You are not a spiritual being having a human experience – there is no being or human.
- The world only appears to be real until you see what it really is and what you really are.

These statements may seem amazing and untrue right now, but I would urge you to remain open as we begin to break down the assumptions that make it seem as though you are living in a solid, tangible world; inside a solid human body that is moving around in time and space. You will be able to take what you read and see if it is true when you apply it. Only then will you see that nothing is the way you have thought it was.

There is just the One and that One is you. You are everywhere at all times and you are not somewhere. Ideas like "somewhere" and "everywhere" don't apply to you if you are formless. Let's stop and check in right now. Take a moment to directly experience the answer to the question "what am I"? and "where am I"? If you notice when you actually experience your true Self you will find you are not a thing, not a form. You can recognise that you are very much here, but where are you actually? Can you even say where you are AND where you are not? Do you have any boundaries?

It is important to rely only on what you can prove to be true and not to go back to thinking about what you are. Notice that your human body and thoughts seem to appear in this vastness that you are – but is that really what is happening? Is there you + your body? In the next few chapters I will challenge these assumptions and you can prove to yourself it is not so and come to see that there is no body, no mind, no thoughts and nothing other than you. It will only be possible to understand these chapters if you are willing to question what you have come to believe in stone as true. It seems very real and logical to most people that they have a human body and they have thoughts – so much so that they probably would never even think to question if it is so in reality. You are reading this book to find out what reality actually is. To do that, you must be willing to question what you may not have questioned before and to look at things in a different way.

The following statements are true. If you let go of all assumptions you will be able to experience them as true. Don't worry if right now they do not feel real to you as yet;

we will work through the assumptions that get in the way of knowing.

I would urge you to read the following statements that are true and notice any resistance to any particular ones. If you find some statements to be difficult to understand, or you understand them logically but cannot seem to live as that, make a note of it. Realising one of these statements to be true will make it easier to understand all of them.

- Being formless means you are effortlessly here.
- Being formless means you are immortal.
- Being formless means there is nothing other than you, different from you or separate from you.
- Being formless means you never, ever, end or begin.
- Being formless means you are unlimited and always have been.
- Being formless means you cannot die and were never born.
- Being formless means you can appear as forms and shapes and objects. Form is not different from formless.
- Being formless means you know everything – because everything is you.
- Being formless means you are infinite. You can never run out of anything, be lacking in anything or want or need anything.

If your experience of life, or reality is different from this, then there are still thoughts and assumptions getting in the way of your perception of reality.

We will look at these statements again and explanations will be given later in the book once we have broken down the assumptions that get in the way. For now, it is enough to know that the highest level of enlightenment is where we live from and as these statements.

Reality is already how it is, nothing is going to change in understanding what you read in this book, but you will simply be finally able to see how it really is and always has been. The world will still appear to be there, your body will still continue to function and do what it needs to do. Everything will remain exactly as it is, but you will be able to see clearly.

The rest of this book will be simply different ways to say the same thing and so I would suggest reading it all at least once and then picking which one fascinates you most and deeply investigating it. Each chapter will help to repeat the fact that form and formless are the same thing, but will approach it from a different angle to help bring to conscious awareness what the assumptions are that are stopping you from seeing this fully.

CHAPTER 4

There Are No Forms Or Objects

Here is a basic error or assumption in our thinking process: "Forms (or things) are real and they are different from and separate from the formlessness."

Here is the fact and what actually is true: There are no objects, there has been no manifestation. Manifestation/the world/all this "out here" is just an illusion of vibration. Tangible and solid is only real in relation to the human senses.

Most human beings would easily and automatically feel that they are sitting in a room that has a certain number of items in it and they are reading this book. Only a few would question if the room was appearing inside themselves. Even fewer people would question which one of these viewpoints is more real and ask, "Am I in the room or is the room in me?"

Occasionally it occurs to someone that the two viewpoints are the same thing, one thing; they are two different perspectives of the one reality. The aim of this book is to help you get to that final realisation and to do so, we have to begin to destroy the concept that objects are real.

There aren't any objects at all. The things you think you see are not there in the way you have thought they were. They only appear to be there and they really are not solid. For something to be real, it must be eternal.

We'll look at two examples of tangible objects and begin to break down the idea that they are real.

Example 1 – A Wooden Table

Let's say you have a wood table in your house. It is safe to say that nearly all of humanity would agree that you have a wooden table which is solid and has dimensions, colour, shape and a lifespan or duration of its existence. They would think anyone who said the table does not exist is a bit crazy!

To begin to grasp the fact that there are no objects or forms we must be willing to think in different ways. When we look at the shape, we see in front of us with our eyes we call it "table" and we believe it is solid and separate from all the other objects in the room, but is it really? If we took a powerful enough microscope and used it to examine the table, we would see it is not so solid at all! First, we would see atoms vibrating and then if we could magnify even more, we would see subatomic particles moving around, appearing and disappearing in front of our eyes.

If we could increase the power of the microscope even more, we would see that underneath the smallest particles was nothing at all! We would eventually come back to the formless and intangible emptiness that is the origin of the table. Whatever "solid" object we put under this microscope would also eventually be seen to be this emptiness, this formless awareness.

Whatever arises out of this awareness MUST be the awareness; even if looks like something completely different from the awareness. When all we start with is that One formlessness (as we proved with our self-enquiry) then how can we suddenly have two things? How can we have the awareness AND a table? We cannot. It can only be that the table is actually the awareness but looks like it is not.

What we have called "table" is really some wood, which is really some atoms, which is really a vibration, which is really the formless Self. The table only seems to be real and solid because we have thought about it, we have sat around it to eat and we have many memories and general thoughts about what we think the table is. We may remember birthday parties, romantic dinners or chats over a cup of tea happening at that table and so we keep the table alive in our own thoughts.

So does the table exist "out there" as a solid lump of wood? No, it does not because it is the awareness in disguise.

Does the table exist "in here" in our thoughts, memories and dreams about it? No, it does not, because those thoughts cease to be when we are in deep sleep, deep meditation or unconscious for any reason. The table vanishes when we do! When we are not here to think about it, the table isn't either!

So why does it appear real to us then? Why is the world so insistent that the table is real and solid? It is because the atoms in it are vibrating at a similar speed to our hands, eyes and senses. When something vibrates at a similar rate to what our human senses can pick up, we call it "solid" and "tangible". We can feel it, it is hard and impacts us if we try to move through it.

If an item is vibrating at a slightly higher level we call it liquid. An even higher vibration and we call it a gas. If something is vibrating very high, it becomes out of the range of our senses. For example, something that vibrates too high for our optic nerves to pick up we call "invisible" (which really means not visible to us). Infrared and ultraviolet light have been proven to exist but they are out of our optic vibrational range and we say they are invisible to the human eye.

We can also see this in the sense of hearing too, as we know there are sounds and pitches that the human ear cannot pick up such as a dog whistle. We call these "inaudible". If we were to use a camera or voice recorder to record a specific period of time and then played it back, we would also hear noises and sounds that we could not pick up using our ears alone.

Human beings all agree that what is tangible and visible to us is real. We believe that what we can see, feel, hear, touch and smell is real and what we cannot use our senses to experience is unreal. We are programmed to ignore the intangible! Consider when the last time was that you noticed the space in a room first (or at all) before the objects you think are in it! Even if you are able to notice the space in a room, consider if you feel on some level that it is less real or important than the objects in the room. Most of us feel sure that the space in the room is different from the objects in it!

To see the reality as it actually is then, we must begin to challenge our familiar ways of thinking. Just because they are very familiar ways to think and everyone agrees with them does not mean they have ever been true. Reality is the formless awareness and it is not vibrating in its ultimate state. Vibration arises from the still awareness and so even vibration must be the awareness too.

Example 2 – A Family Member (e.g. my brother)

For the second example we will look at an object that appears to be external to ourselves and has great emotional value and meaning to us. You can substitute brother with sister, mother or father if you prefer. Most people again would agree that your brother is a real thing and that he has a life of his own separate from yours. Some people would agree that we are all one and so their brother must be the same as them. Few people would want to question if their brother and themselves were even real. You are one of those people. How do I know that? I know it because you are reading this book.

What is a "brother" anyway? What I could call brother is really a human body that my mother gave birth to just like she did me. But "brother" cannot really just be a human body; it must be something else. Where does my brother exist? Is he "out there" as a man I interact with and share parents with? Or is he "in here" as a thought, an idea and a familiar set of memories involving one particular person? Is my brother both of these or neither?

First we will look at the "out there" part in which my brother seems to be someone I see and can hug or even argue with. But that human body is not really a body; it is a bunch of organs, blood, tissues and bone. When we look even closer those tissues and organs become cells and if we look even closer we find molecules and DNA. If we look even closer, what we have called "my brother" is really a product of all the food my mother ate when she was pregnant and all the

21

food my brother ate since birth. We could even say that what I have called my brother is simply food!

"Brother" could also be seen as the product of a sperm and an ovum from my parents and my parents are really just the product of two more sperms and ova. And so on it goes. The sperm and the egg (as well as anything else) can be seen under a microscope to be simply vibration and if we look closer, can be seen to be simply the formlessness.

Now the point of all this is not to depress you, but to help you come to see that what you have valued as a separate, real and dependable thing is not really so. As human beings, we like to find other humans that make us feel safer such as family members, friends and romantic partners. We keep telling ourselves they are outside and different from us, but it is never so. You are the formlessness and you do not end. What you consider to be external to you, really is not. There is nothing external or separate from you.

What about the "in here" part of your brother? Inside my mind my brother can exist in a way based on all the thoughts I have about him and the time we have spent together and how I think and feel about him. He exists as a set of thoughts and emotions and memories I think I have had based on the idea he is separate from me and I have a relationship with him. Can that relationship exist in reality if there is only me? All of the meaning, value and worth I put on my brother is really derived from the way the thoughts and memories in my head of him make me feel.

Today, I may argue with my brother and so my thoughts about him will be different from they were yesterday when I felt happy to be with him. As my brother grows and changes my thoughts about him change too and so even the idea I have of him is constantly changing and not stable (just as my ideas about myself are too).

We can do this with every single person in our lives and come to the same conclusion that they really do not exist as separate entities no matter how much we have wanted to believe they do. Once we begin to see that they are inside of us and they ARE us, we will no longer be able to externalise them and we will not be broken if they leave us or pass away.

It is good practise too to see that the body you so highly value as yourself is actually a sperm and an egg and some borrowed DNA from your parents. When you eat a sandwich it is digested and becomes a part of your body. When exactly did it stop being a sandwich and when did it become a human body? When did it stop being a sandwich and when did it start being "me"? If we continue to think this way for even a short while, it will allow us to begin to dissolve the idea that objects we have valued most dearly are really there at all. What we have valued is how those imagined objects make us feel.

You may find this very shocking, weird or strange to think about, but let's remember that you are simply finding out how this has always been. You are coming to see what reality has always been. I am simply helping you to break down what you have assumed was true and to find the courage to let go of some of your most prized assumptions.

CHAPTER 5

The Difference Between the Subject and An Object

Here is a basic error or assumption in our thinking process: "I know what subjective means, and subjective can include objects inside it that are separate from it. I have fully seen what it means to be the subjective Self. I know what the Self is."

Here is the fact and what actually is true: True subjectivity excludes any possibility of objectivity and there are no objects in the subjective. We think we are an object that comes and goes. What we actually are is pure subjectivity devoid of any objects. The subject and object are the SAME thing. They are one.

When we self-enquire and directly experience what we are we find no thing that we can call "me". There is a stillness of course, a sense of "I am here" which is more subjective. We must come to see that if we have believed that we are a separate being that we are really still seeing ourselves as an object. We can perceive our sense of being someone because it is made up of thoughts, emotions, memories, dreams and expectations. These are constantly changing and coming and going. This sense of self fits the category of "object" more than subjective awareness because it disappears completely in deep meditation, in deep sleep, when unconscious or under anaesthetic. What we have come to call "me" is really an object that is coming and going every night and day and disappears each time we are not thinking about anything. We can recall also from the previous chapter that most of what we call "me" is made up of thoughts about other people that we think are separate from us.

Truly subjective experiencing is the only thing we can be sure of when we self-enquire. There is a sense "I am here" and we cannot find exactly where that is located. If you really look right now, you will see that you cannot find where that sense of you stops. It has no boundaries. That means you go on forever.

I will say that again because it may seem so amazing and may be hard to comprehend at first.

If you cannot find where you end, then you must go on forever and you must be the unlimited being.

You are the infinite Self which is everywhere all the time but you have become so used to perceiving yourself as being limited and only located here. So can you be the infinite Self and go on forever but have a lot of holes inside you where the objects of your perception seem to be? Is there a gap in your infinite subjective Self where your brother is? Is he separate to your awareness?

Can you even have a gap in an infinite being? No, you cannot – because it would not be infinite then. There can be no places you are not and there can be no places you are absent. All these "other" beings are you and all these objects are also you. There is nothing outside of you.

The dictionary definition of infinite is: "limitless or endless in space, extent or size, impossible to measure or calculate". So if you think there are over 7 billion human beings and countless billions of animal and insect species then that would make you an infinite being with holes inside you that are too numerous to count. If you spend even a few minutes thinking about this you will see it must all be you. Even if we consider something smaller and more local, we can see it is not so. Consider the sofa you are sitting on right now or the clothes you are wearing that seem separate from you – are they really? How far does your infinite being go?

I have seen many students tell me they know what it is to be formless but they imagine a human body sitting less than two metres away is separate from them and the air around them is also separate. To know what it is to be formless is really to accept there is nothing outside of you, different from you or separate from you. It may look as though you are just a human being living in a world populated by countless beings and insentient things, but this cannot be so. It really is a choice now of where you want to live from. You must either choose to live as that infinite being that you are OR continue imagining yourself to be small and limited and here only for a short time.

Even to say you will have to choose is not really true because as you continue to read and digest what you learn in this book you will come to see that this has always been so.

So what is actually happening then? Why do we keep imagining that all these other beings or objects exist in addition to us? It is really due to one simple error in our thinking process. We treat the subjective awareness as if it were an object and we give it the properties of an object.

We believe that the subjective Self is displaced, moved or replaced by an object. Because we believe that it must be one or the other (subjective Self OR object) we feel that when we see an object, it must have taken the place of the subjective awareness or pushed it out of the way. We must come to see that the Self is subjective and has no definable qualities like an object does. It is not hard or soft, long or short, big or small. The Self has no edges that would push up against an object. If we take an example of empty space and put a cup in that space have we moved or displaced the space? No we haven't at all. Formless awareness does not have anything tangible about it to shove up against and not even an atomic bomb or hurricane could cause the formlessness to move out of the way to allow space for an object to occupy that space. Formlessness is infinite and in all places at all times and so where would it go anyway, if it were moved? Can you move something that is already everywhere and not able to be nowhere? Deeply contemplating the truths you have read here will allow you to begin to live from them and as them. You must keep interested in this subject until you are convinced that what you read is true and you can prove it to your own self in your experience. You cannot prove this is true to anyone else and you do not need to. Once you are convinced of this you will feel at peace and you will directly experience reality for the first time.

The objects and the subject must be the same thing if they are in the same place.

Subject and object cannot even be two things, because that would again imply there is somewhere that the subjective Self is missing or absent from. This means that everything we perceive as an object, separate from myself and different from me, cannot actually be so. All objects are not really objects but are the Subjective Self appearing to be different.

Appearing to be different than the Self is not *actually* different.

CHAPTER 6

The Difference Between the Noumenon and Phenomena. What is Real and Unreal?

First, we must begin by explaining and defining what "Noumenon" and "phenomena" mean:

The **Noumenon** is something which exists outside of AND is undetectable by the human senses. It is not something that can be experienced by us as something that comes and goes because it is not perceptible by our five senses. It is most certainly NOT the opposite to phenomena.

A **phenomenon** is something that can be observed as existing. It can be experienced by our senses and it can be thought about in our mind. A phenomenon is an object of our perception.

Here is a basic error or assumption in our thinking process: "The Noumenon and a phenomenon are opposites. All the phenomena exist inside the Noumenon."

Here is the fact and what actually is true: There aren't any phenomena because they simply appear to exist inside the Noumenon. The Noumenon is all pervading so all phenomena are made out of it and ARE it. The Noumenon has no opposite. It is one and is beyond all duality. The Noumenon and phenomena are the same One and only appear to be different.

As we learned in the previous chapters, we are conditioned to value only that which we can perceive with our five human senses or that we can think about. Our mind thinks about the objects we perceive with our senses because it thinks they are real. Once we have come to see that our true essence is the formless Self, we will tend to reject the forms or the phenomena that we see.

To realise the ultimate state of reality it is necessary to stop trying to distinguish which is most real. As spiritual students we had to develop an ability to discriminate between "real and unreal" or "truth and illusion" and this was very necessary until now. In this final seeing, we must come to realise that if we are trying to decide which is most real, we will be excluding something else. Our journey of realisations usually goes something like this:

Step 1 – "I am this body".
Here we are convinced that we are a separate being that was born and will die. We are excluding everything else that exists in our definition of "me" and "what I am".

Step 2 – "I am not this body".
Here we come to realise that we are not limited to the body, we are formless in our nature and we identify as that formless Self or awareness. We feel strongly that we are NOT any

form, any manifestation and we dismiss anything transient, temporary and changing as unreal. We can become very detached in this step from our mind, body and our life.

Step 3 – "I am the formless Self and all that arises out of it". In this step, we have come to see that anything which has arisen out of the Self must be the Self also. We now include all objects and forms in our definition of what we are. We may say or believe something like "I am the formless Awareness and all that arises from it is me also."

The important thing to note in this step is that although we may have included all form back into our self-definition (what we know ourselves to be) we are still seeing form and formless as different. The vital point to understand here, is that I may still think of myself as two different things. We may say the manifest arises out of the unmanifest source; or that all of this creation arises out of the creator. We could also believe in God vs Godhead.

We must come to see that even this level of realisation will cause us to suffer eventually because it is still seeing TWO different things. We are still discriminating between "real" which is the Noumenon or formless Self and what we think of as "unreal" which is the phenomena that we see coming and going.

If we stop for a moment and directly experience what we are, we will find only One in that direct experience. Let me caution you again here against *thinking* about the Self. Of course, you will have to use your mind to understand what is written here, but to check it against your own direct experience, you must actually look with your inner sight to see what you actually are.

It is vitally important to confirm in your own experience and to prove to yourself that you cannot find two when you look. There is just you – only One. Confirm this over and over.

There is a lot of literature and scripture written about steps 1, 2, and 3 but this book is written to clearly explain step 4. The final stage of realisation has rarely been clearly explained and all of this book is dedicated to that.

Step 4 of Self-realisation is when we simply do not know what we are. We have no idea at all what we are and we have no interest in any self-definition. To define what we are would only be happening at the level of thought and it would automatically exclude something from that definition.

The very moment I know what I am, then I create the opposite in my experience and I must experience it over and over. If I know I am formless, then I will keep having experiences of being a particular form. If I know I am a form, I will keep having experiences of being formless (what the world calls death, birth and life). The very moment I know I am both form and formless, I must keep having wild swings in my experience of being form and formless. I will experience the small contracted state of being a human being only and then massive expansion back to being infinite and everywhere. I will keep switching back to from one to the other in an endless cycle of expansion and contraction experiences.

If I know that formlessness is real and forms are unreal, then I am still seeing TWO items there and will have to continue to experience in dualistic ways and suffer.

I can only come to see that form and formless are the same thing and that both words are synonyms for Reality.

Form is the formlessness appearing to be a shape. Formlessness IS the essence of all forms.

Step 4 then becomes "I have no idea what I am, what God is, what Reality is. I am beyond any definition. I have no ability to determine, discriminate or label and I am totally happy".

It really is as simple as not thinking about yourself at all OR knowing that no thought is going to be true about you. Even the thought "I am the All" or "I am Nothing" is not true here. You do not need to eliminate thoughts or stop the mind working. It is enough to see no thought about you, or anything at all, has ever been true.

"I am ALL" is not true because the concept of "all" includes numerous forms and categories. There are no objects, manifestation has never truly occurred as something independent to the Self.

"I am Nothing" is also not true because it excludes all forms and objects.

Even to feel that both of these are true or neither of them are is still delusion and self-defining.

CHAPTER 7

One Final Note

If you read this book and have a sense that what you have understood from it is real and what you knew before you read it is unreal then you have not totally understood what the noumenon is. The Self is totally inclusive of all levels of consciousness and all understanding.

If I strongly believe myself to be a limited person, separate and alone, moving through this lifetime and trying to find happiness before I die, then I will experience that as absolutely real. It will be so real to me that all my experiences will verify it as true. It will not even occur to me to question if there could be more to see, unless I start to have a very negative experience of being a separate being. Even at that point, I may still be so convinced that what I know is true that I may turn away from an authentic spiritual teacher or teaching, calling them crazy or just plain wrong.

If I come to realise that I am the unmanifest Self and I am beyond all form that will also seem totally real to me too.

If I realise I am both the form and formless then that will seem completely and absolutely real to me.

How can all these "levels" of reality be true for me? How is the next person's belief in having been born and living their life as real as what I have seen? It is simply that I am Reality (what that is I do not know!) and anything I am experiencing anywhere from any point of view must be reality experiencing itself. Any experience I have in any human body (or any animal, plant or "insentient" item) is totally and absolutely real because I am Reality.

Whatever I believe to be true is immediately true for me. Whatever I know and am certain is real will be experienced as real to me. As the One Reality I am all-pervading and therefore all of my viewpoints are equally valid. If I exclude any one of them at all I am defining and I am limiting myself again.

It is natural to want to live as the Absolute Reality because that is the only place we will not suffer or feel limited in any way at all; but we must not exclude anything at all in that realisation.

APPENDIX

Summary of Common Names For the Noumenon

Below are some of the ways the Noumenon has been described in other teachings. For each set of terms there are two names. Reading through the list may help to awaken a recognition in you as you read and at certain times along the way different sets of terms may be more appealing than others.

They are all names for That Which Has No Name. Don't get attached to any name; look at what the name points to.

NOUMENON	PHENOMENA
Oneness	many
Allness	separation
Empty Mind	full mind
Unity	multiplicity
Silent Mind	noisy mind
Non-Duality	duality

"I" as Consciousness	"I" as a person
Nothingness	somethingness
Awakeness	sleep/dream
Consciousness	unconsciousness
Silence	sound
Subjectivity	object
Being	being someone/something
Stillness	movement
Presence	person
God	ego
Truth	falsehood
Formless	form
Reality	illusion
Knowingness	knowing about
Awareness	perception
Context	content
Infinite Field	finite being
Timeless	duration

If you would like more information about Helen, her live Satsangs, silent retreats and classes please contact us:

Visit the website at **www.helenhamilton.org**

Find us on Facebook by searching: @satsangwithhelenhamilton

Find us on YouTube by searching "Satsang With Helen Hamilton"

Email the Satsang with Helen Hamilton team at evolution ofspirit@gmail.com

Printed in Great Britain
by Amazon

17259346R00030